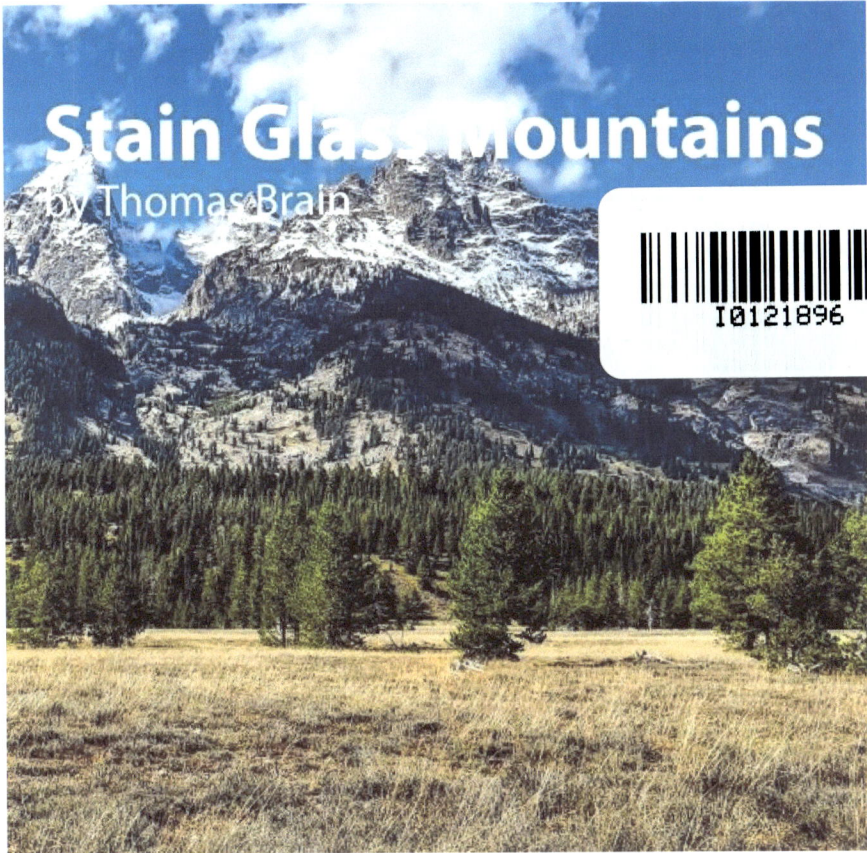

Stain Glass Mountains
by Thomas Brain

1

Stain Glass Mountains

Thomas Brain Publisher
1657 Red Oak Lane Rockford, Illinois 61107

Stain Glass Mountains

Printed in the United States of America

Order books from your local bookstore referencing the ISBN below or contact the author through his website
http://.thomasbrainphotography.com
tombrain1@aol.com

ISBN: 978-0-578-89287-0

This humble book is dedicated to my partner that has followed me down this dusty path for over fifty years. My complete love and admiration. To our greatest gifts, two ever growing and excelling sons. Tyler and Elliott

Sadi: The honest, smart, hardworking, caring, example of motherhood.

Ellie: education, athletics and the arts are awaiting to watch your dreams come true.

Emmie: The science field is waiting for you to become part of the engineering team that builds the habitats for mars.

Mark and Liz, Thank you for showing us more of natures storybook.

Support the fight against cancer.
In Remebrance:
Doris Brain, June Simon, Cathy Downing, Johnny Kasch

The Eagles wing beckons us home. come in only to see. Hear the wispering comfort of the Stain Glass Tree.

Does the earth smile in flowers?

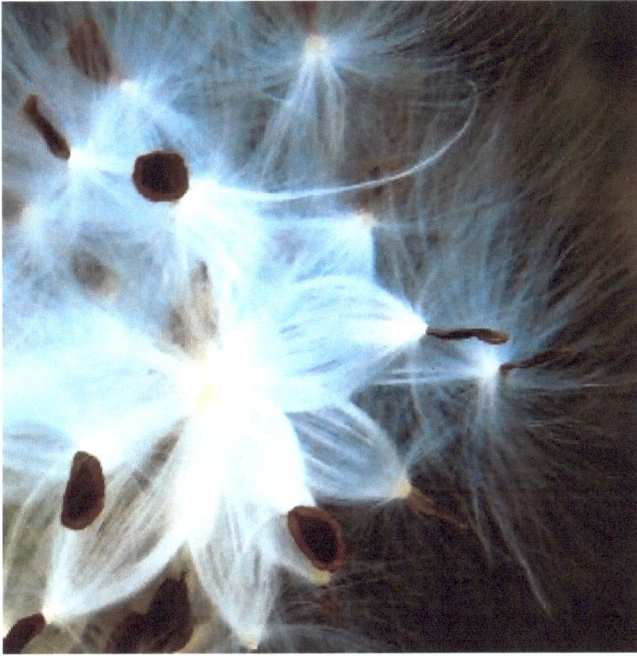

The softness of the Milkweed.

Find the clouds. Find the sun. It is life's story.

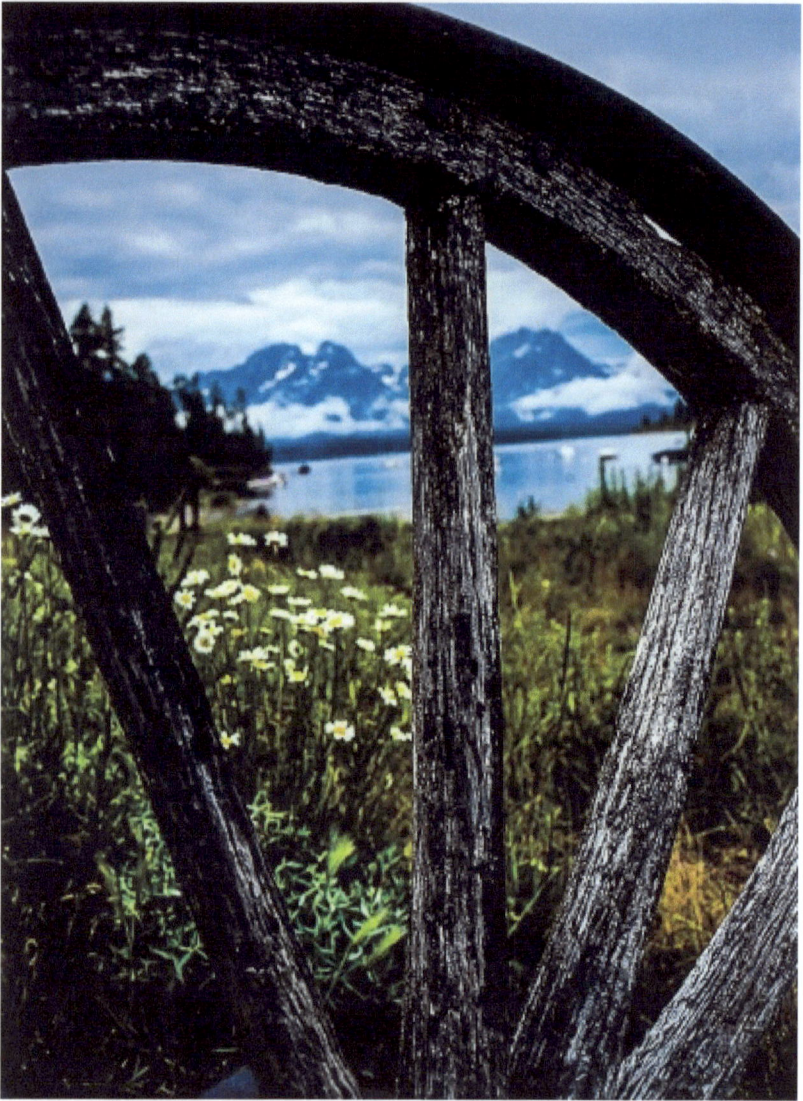

The beauty is there for all to see.

Place those special days high on
the shelf of memories.

The Honesty of Silence.

Welcome come in beckons the eagle.

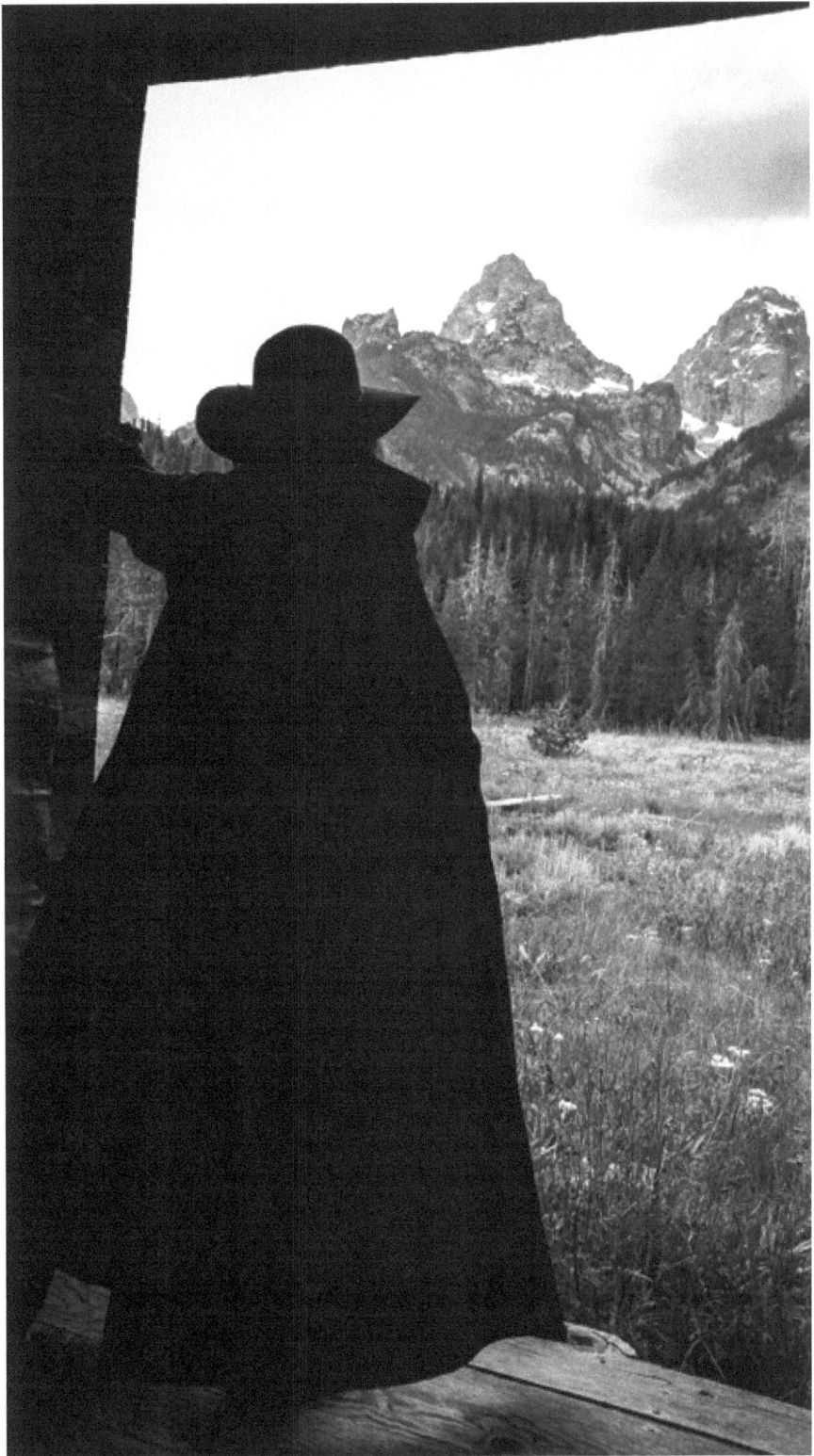

The invisible summons of ancient DNA.

When you reach that spot that is all wonderment.

A gift only for you.

What is beauty?

Can you hear the silence?

Listen closely to the quiet.

Maude Nobles Cabin

A meeting in this cabin in 1923 put in motion the establishment of the Grand Teton Park.

Can you hear the first dusty leather boots on the wooden floor?

Going to the Sun

Smell the sweet taste of cold clean
air at 6641 ft.

The Art of Nature.

*From Cyrstal to liquid the
sparkling gold hurries down its*

slide. Say hello and then good bye.

A small growth to say the season of sun is soon to come. A wider wooden ring in the tallest of calenders.

The Majestic roam in their forest home.

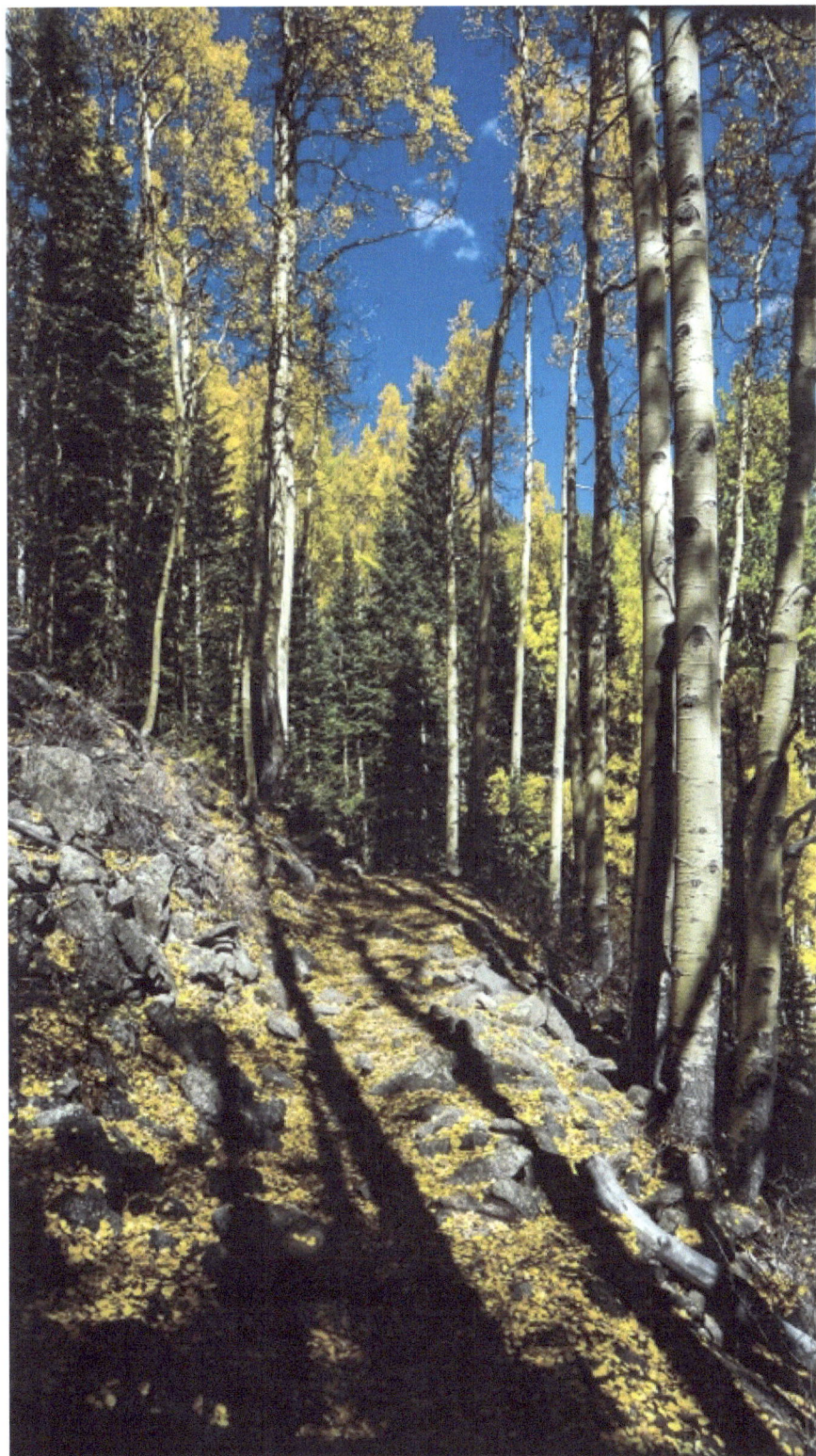

The hypontic quaking of that
special wooden spire that waits
for the smallest of breaths.

With Hesitency it releases its
miniature golden flags for only
the honored to see.

*A dolip of sand, crystal cold h2o, crisp
mountain air.*

Blend very slowly.

Savor in small portions for as long as possible.

*Do we find **ourselves** by looking into the soul of **nature?***

*The dig of the trek poles replenishes the **soul**.*

A journey will change with each footstep.
Just take the next one.

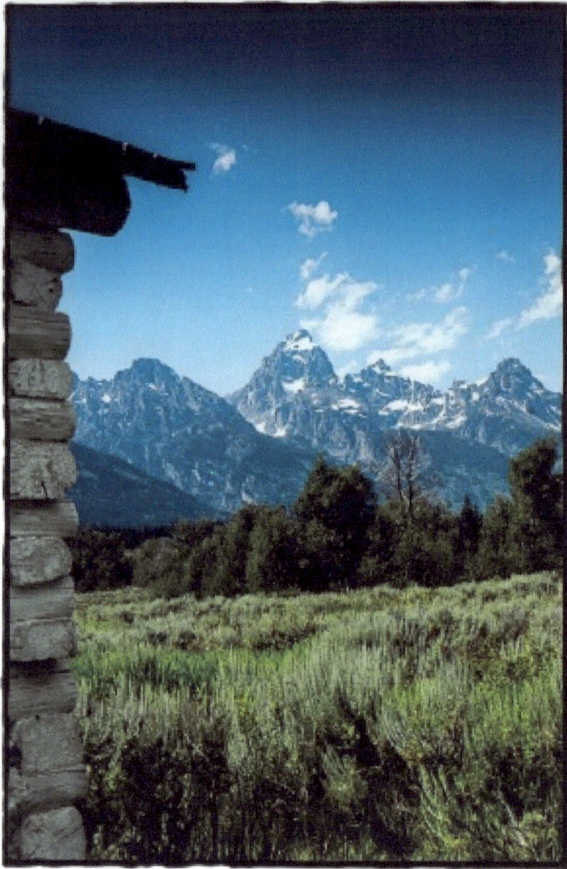

Around every corner is another
memory.

The smell of forest.

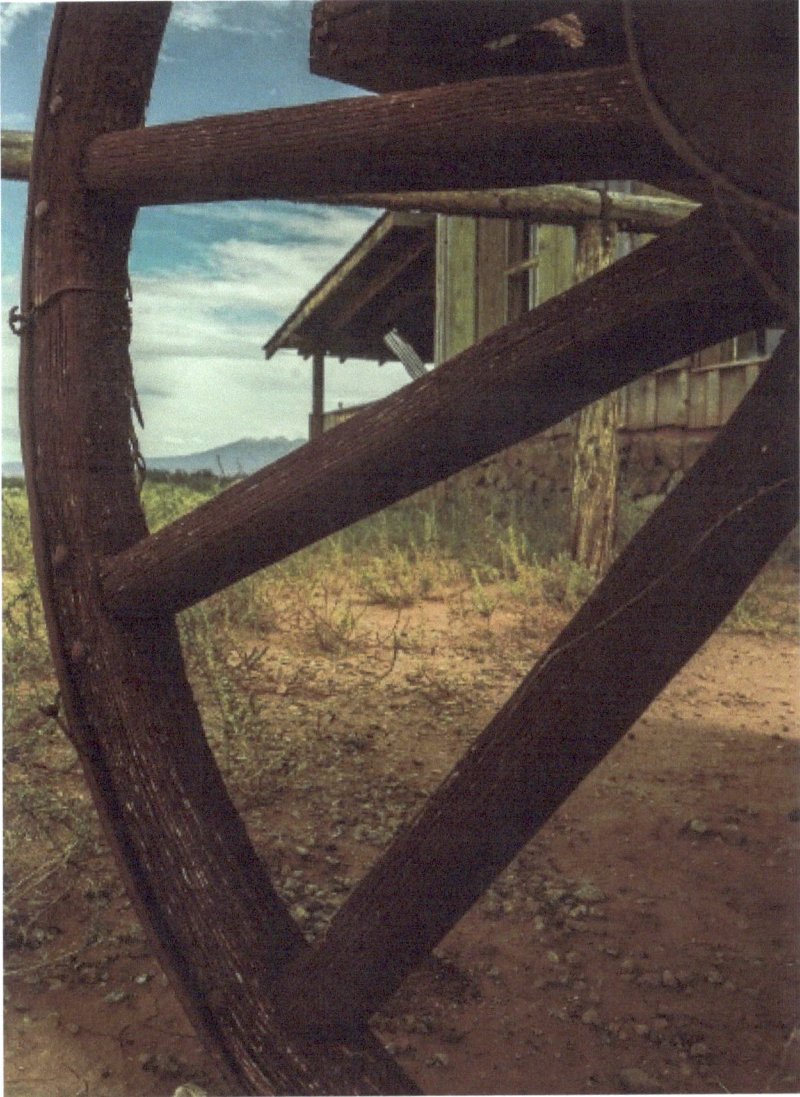

Can we see the past in the present?

It is all in how you look at **Life**.

The flower of the Monarch Butterfly.

The beauty is there for you to find.

The only photograph of a snowball race.

The Doris Rose.

Hear the roar. Feel the spray.

It is the journey.

Being part of nature.

Stain Glass Mountains

Photographs & thoughts by Thomas Brain

Is there still a whiff of a
campfire from long ago? The
original renters of this land
were witnesses to the
thundering herds of tatanka,
clouds of winged colors as the
seasons turned to another.
Be respectful of their legacy.

Your thoughts, notes and sketchs

What do you see, smell, and hear?